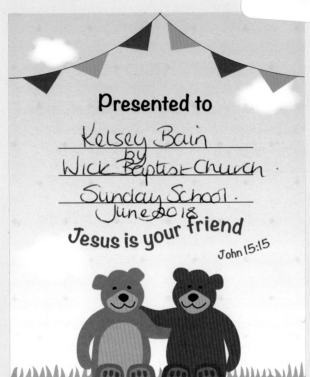

Presented to

Kelsey Bain
by
Wick Baptist Church.
Sunday School.
June 2018

Jesus is your friend

John 15:15

NICK BUTTERWORTH AND MICK INKPEN

ANIMAL TALES

NICK BUTTERWORTH AND MICK INKPEN
ANIMAL TALES

CANDLE
BOOKS

USA edition published by Zonderkidz ®

Published by Candle Books
an imprint of
Lion Hudson plc
Wilkinson House, Jordan Hill Road,
Oxford OX2 8DR, England
www.lionhudson.com/candle

ISBN 978 1 85985 637 6

First edition 2006

A catalogue record for this book is available from the British Library

Printed and bound in China, August 2017, LH54

Contents

THE FOX'S TALE

JESUS IS BORN

Hello, I'm a fox. I live out on the hills. I sleep by day and hunt by night.

If you're lucky you might see me on a hilltop against the moon. But don't blink or I'll be gone.

Here's my story. It'll make your tail bristle. Listen.

Two nights ago I'm up on the hill
near the town. The night is cold and
clear. I lift my head and sniff the air.
The scent of sheep is everywhere.

There's another smell too. It halts me
in my tracks. The shepherd's out…
by my nose more than one. That means
the sheep are lambing.

I skirt around the hill, then wait a while, and listen. Somewhere up ahead a lamb is calling to its mother.

Crouching low and keeping to the bushes I follow. Now I can see it clearly sitting in the long grass. A speckled lamb, not one week old.

Suddenly a blinding flash sends me running to the bushes. Shaking to my toes and blinking in the light, I freeze.

Across the hill a golden glow has fallen. And coming from the sky the sound of singing.

All at once the air is filled with shining men!

I'm scared. I cannot smell these men. They have no scent.

One of them is speaking to the shepherds.

'Don't be afraid,' he says. 'We bring good news. Great joy has come to all of you. Today in Bethlehem a baby has been born. He is your promised King, your Saviour. You'll find him lying in a cattle trough. Quickly, run and see!'

Suddenly, the shining men are gone. The sound of singing dies away.

The shepherds stare at one another. Then all at once they start to talk.

They laugh and shout. They jump and clap their hands. Then off they run towards the town to find the baby King. I follow on behind.

I am wary of the town. It's full of sounds and smells I do not know. But I would like to see this baby King.

Keeping to the shadows I watch the shepherds disappear inside a stable.

Behind the stable is a high fence.
Without a sound I'm up and over it.

My luck is in. There is light
streaming through a crack in the back
wall. From here I can see everything.

Inside are cows and sheep and goats. It's odd. They know I'm here but they are not afraid.

There are people too. A woman and a man, and by the door the shepherds. All of them are looking at a cattle trough lit by a lantern.

And there, just as the shining men said, a newborn baby sleeps. A King in a cattle shed.

His mother smiles and tells the shepherds to come in. Quietly they stand and watch. The baby murmurs in his sleep.

'His name is Jesus,' says the woman softly.

One of the shepherds takes something from his cloak. It is the speckled lamb. A present for the baby.

He gives it to the woman, then bends close to see the baby's face.

The shepherd's smiling face glows in the light, just like the shining men. He has seen a King and so have I. Not many shepherds or foxes can say that.

The shepherds whisper their goodbyes and leave.

My belly tells me that I too must be making tracks. It is a harsh winter and life is hard for a fox. And for you too, little King, it seems.

I wish you well. I hope the lamb will keep you warm. Sweet dreams.

THE CAT'S TALE

JESUS AT THE WEDDING

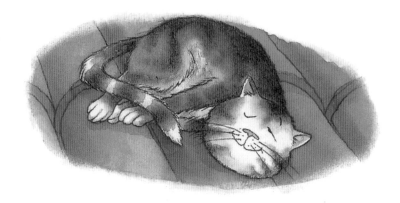

Hello, I'm the cat who lives next door at number three. I expect you've seen me sunning myself up here on the roof. I like it up here. I can keep an eye on things.

I was up here the other day when a truly amazing thing happened. I knew something was up the moment I saw the servants sweeping the courtyard…

There I am watching them get ready
for the party. Someone's getting married
and everyone's been invited. It's going
to be the party of the year.

Down below the servants are hurrying
about with tables and chairs.

'Put them here,' says the Steward.
He is the man in charge.

Now out comes the food.

What a feast! There are pies and cakes and roasted meat, all kinds of fish and loaves of bread, there are pots of honey, flasks of wine and bowls piled high with nuts and grapes.

I curl my tail and lick my lips. A piece of fish would be nice.

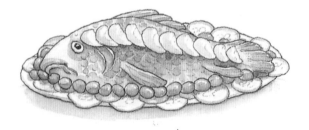

Soon the guests arrive. One or two at first, then lots more, streaming through the gate, laughing and chattering.

One of them is called Jesus. He's come with a big crowd. When he speaks everyone gathers round and listens.

I knew something was going to happen the moment I set eyes on him.

Now everyone is here. The party
can begin. I'll go down and hide under
one of the tables. Maybe I'll sit on
someone's lap and purr for scraps
of food.

Everyone is happy. Everyone is laughing and joking. Everyone has a story to tell. Everyone is enjoying the party. Everyone except one woman.

I can hear her talking to her friend.

'Mary! Whatever shall we do? The wine is running out and we've only just begun. What can we give them all to drink? The party will be ruined.'

'I'll have a word with Jesus,' says the other woman. She hurries to his table and whispers in his ear. I follow on behind, ears pricked.

Standing in the courtyard are six huge stone jars.

'Quickly!' says Jesus to the servants, 'fill these jars with water.'

Water? What good is water at a wedding? Wine is what we need, not water.

The servants do as they are told. Off to the well and back again, with buckets, jugs and leather bottles.

Splish! Splash! Backwards and forwards until the jars are full.

One hundred and fifty gallons! Thirsty work.

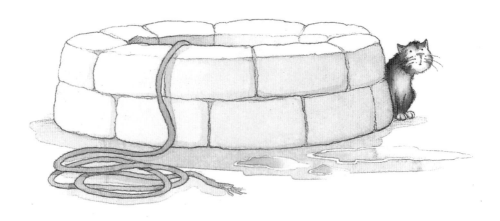

'Now draw some off,' says Jesus, 'and drink.'

The woman dips a pitcher in, and then she gasps! There in her hand is not the water that the servants brought, but dark red wine!

Wine! Enough for everyone to drink and come again.

The Steward tastes the wine and says, 'The best was saved till last!' And everybody cheers and passes round the jug.

So much excitement in one day. I'm off to sleep away the afternoon.

I curl up on the roof, and soon I'm dreaming.

When I wake up it's growing dark. The guests have gone. The moon is up. Did the water change to wine or was it all a dream? Looking down I see the jars and one of them is still half full. The moon's reflection in the jar is pink!

So Jesus really turned the water into wine. What an amazing man. We've not heard the last of him. I'd bet my whiskers on it.

THE MAGPIE'S TALE

JESUS AND ZACCHAEUS

Hello, I'm a magpie. I live in this sycamore tree.

You see the gold ring I'm holding in my beak? I found it. Well, I pinched it really. I used to have lots of stolen things in this nest. Not any more.

Let me tell you the story. It all began yesterday afternoon…

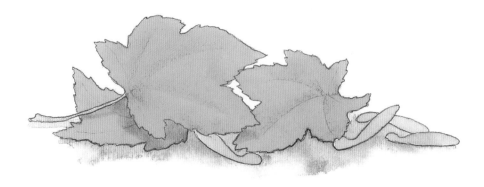

It's a hot day and I'm sitting out of the sun guarding my stolen treasure.

Suddenly I hear the sound of people laughing.

Down below a large crowd is gathering. That's odd. Usually nothing happens around here in the middle of the afternoon.

The people have lined up along the street. They seem to be waiting for someone. I wonder who it is. He must be important.

Look, even Zacchaeus has come out to see. He's the short, fat man who lives in the big house on the corner. Nobody likes him much. He collects the taxes. They say he's a cheat.

Zacchaeus is too short to see over
the crowd. He's trying to push his way
to the front. But he's too fat to squeeze
through, and the people won't let
him past.

They're pretending not to notice
him at all. Nobody likes Zacchaeus.

Now he's coming over to my tree.
He's climbing up to get a better view!
But his short legs won't reach the
branches. He's puffing and panting and
going red in the face.

Quickly! The important man will be
here soon! Go on Zacchaeus, you can
do it!

Just in time Zacchaeus scrambles into the tree. The crowd starts to cheer and everybody presses forward.

'Hooray, here comes Jesus!'

I can just see his face through the leaves. But who is Jesus? He doesn't look important at all. Not like a King, or a General.

By the look of him, he's not even rich. Just an ordinary man.

Jesus walks up to my tree, stops
and looks up through the branches.
Perhaps he has spotted my treasure
sparkling in the sun.

Does he know I stole it? What does
he want?

'Zaccheus, come down,' says Jesus with a laugh. 'I'd like to stay at your house today.'

Zaccheus nearly falls off his branch. What a surprise. Why would anyone want to stay with Zaccheus? Nobody likes Zaccheus.

Zacchaeus climbs down and Jesus says hello. It's very strange. He speaks to Zacchaeus like an old friend.

The crowd don't like it at all.

'Why choose Zacchaeus? He's a cheat and a thief!' says one woman.

Now Zacchaeus speaks out loud,
for everyone to hear.

'I'll give half of everything I own
away,' he says, 'and everyone I've
cheated I'll pay back four times over.'

The people are amazed. What has
happened to Zacchaeus? He's like a
different man.

Since then I've taken back everything
I stole. The things from my nest have
been turning up all over town!

This golden ring is all that's left.
I pinched it from the big house on
the corner. Zacchaeus left it on the
window sill.

He'll be pleased to get it back,
I should think.

THE MOUSE'S TALE

JESUS AND THE STORM

Hello, I'm a mouse, a ship's mouse. And this is my house. It's a fishing boat.

In the evening, when the fishermen have gone home, that's when I wake up. I come out and sniff and nibble the fishing nets.

Well, the other evening, a strange thing happened.

I'm nosing about on deck as usual when suddenly, there's a noise. Quick as a flash I hide behind some old ropes.

Listen, there are footsteps! The fishermen have come back. Twitch my whiskers and sniff the air. There's someone with them.

I can hear the fishermen untying the boat. Splish splash. I can feel them pushing it out into the waves. The wind catches the sail, the mast creaks, the boat rocks gently and we're heading out to sea.

'It's been a long day,' says a voice I don't know. 'I think I'll get some sleep.'

Where are we going? We're not going fishing. It's too late for fishing. Where are we going?

We're taking the man with the voice I don't know for a ride in our boat.

The man sits down right next to me and leans his head on my ropes. His hair smells warm. He's not a fisherman.

Everything is quiet except for the waves slapping under the boat.

Soon the man is asleep. I want a better look at him. I creep out from under the ropes. All clear.

The man looks very tired. He has a kind face and he snores.

His breath tickles my whiskers. He can ride in our boat if he likes. I wonder what his name is.

All of a sudden – Flash! Bang! I'm off and running.

Flash! Bang! Lightning and thunder! I scamper up the deck and down my hole.

Flash! Bang! We're in for a rough ride. These summer storms can be nasty.

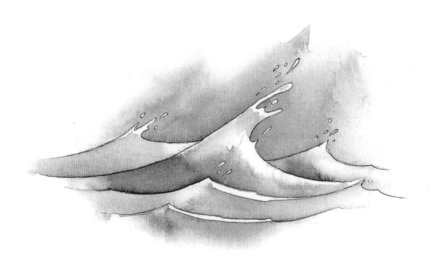

Now the great black clouds close in. The sky grows dark.

Big drops of rain begin to splatter on the deck. The sail flaps and bangs and gulps the wind.

The storm whips spray across the deck and giant waves slam the boat.

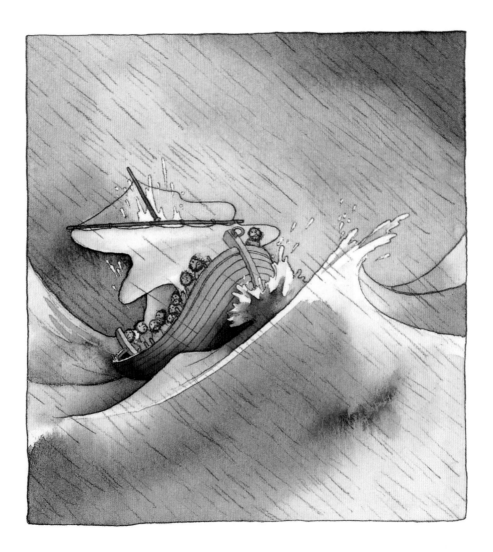

The boat begins to roll and slide.

One moment up, next moment down. Up and down, up and down with water crashing on the deck and pouring on my head.

And all the while – Flash! Bang! Lightning and thunder. And all the while – Slap! Crack! The wind tatters our sail. And all the while the man sleeps on … and snores.

'Wake up! Wake up! We're going to sink! Wake up! Wake up! We'll all be drowned! Wake up! Wake up! We're going down! Jesus, wake up!'

So that's his name.

Slowly, the man opens his eyes. He blinks and rubs his face and looks around.

And holding on the mast, he stands up straight.

Then stretching out his hand he shouts into the wind.

His voice is firm and strong and very, very loud.

'Peace!' he shouts. 'Be still!'

And straight away the storm does what he tells it to!

The wind dies down, the thunder stops, the sea is calm and all is still.

Can you believe it? The wind, the lightning, thunder, waves and rain all stop! What kind of man is that?

The setting sun peeps out behind a cloud. The men get out the oars to row us home. I shake the water from my paws and ears and settle down to sleep.

So pull the oars, we'll soon be home to tell the tale.

And that man Jesus, if he wants to, he can sail with us again.

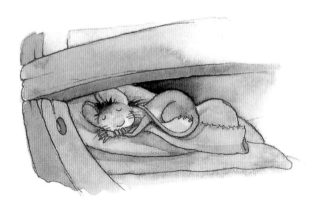